Contents

Macmillan Education
4 Crinan Street
London N1 9XW
A division of Springer Nature Limited

Companies and representatives throughout the world

Ferris Wheel 3 Activity Book ISBN 978-1-380-01871-7

First published 2019

Original design by Clare Webber
Page make-up by emc design ltd
Illustrated by Jose Ignacio Gómez (Nacho Gómez) pp3–84 (all character artwork and main illustrations)
Other illustrations by BluBlu Animation Group Sp. z o.o. pp.3b, 4t, 9, 10–12, 13b, 14, 20tr, bl, br, 23b, 28, 33b, 34, 39t, 41, 43b, 60, 61, 63b, 70, 73b, 80, 83b, 85–96; Conor Rawson (Beehive Illustration) pp20tl, 22, 30, 32, 40, 42, 62, 72, 82.
Cover design by emc design ltd
Cover illustration by Jose Ignacio Gómez (Nacho Gómez)

Authors' acknowledgements
I would like to thank everyone at Macmillan Education in the UK, Spain and Mexico who has contributed to the development and production of these materials. I would also like to thank all the teachers who have taken time to read and pilot the materials, and given invaluable feedback at every stage of writing the course. Special thanks as ever go to my husband, Alan, for his encouragement and support, and to our son and daughter, Jamie and Hannah, from whose early childhood days I learnt so much.

The publishers would like to thank Alex Tamulis, São Paulo, Brazil; Ayşegül Sezer, İNO Schools, Turkey; Daniela Araujo Pielli, Alt Idiomas, São Bernardo Do Campo, Brazil; Daniela Pugliese, Milton's College, Buenos Aires, Argentina; Esra Ezici, Turkey; Fernanda Domeniconi Nery Amorim, São Paulo, Brazil; Gabriela Iocolari, English Schoolhouse, Buenos Aires, Argentina; Gulbin Cin, Bahcesehir College, Turkey; Mariana Pastorino, Em Pi Instituto de Inglés, Santa Fe, Argentina; Mariné Ortiz, Warrington, Buenos Aires, Argentina; Paola Daniela Tuninetti, Academia Argüello, Córdoba, Argentina; Silvana Paola Accardo, Escuela Cooperativa Mundo Nuevo Instituto Casa de Jesús, Buenos Aires, Argentina.

Printed and bound in Brazil

2025
46

Hello
How are you?

Vocabulary Lesson 1

Point and say the names. Trace the numbers and say. Color the Ferris Wheel and say the colors. Language: Mommy, Daddy, Mimi, Dylan; Ferris Wheel; blue, green, orange, pink, red, yellow; numbers 1–6

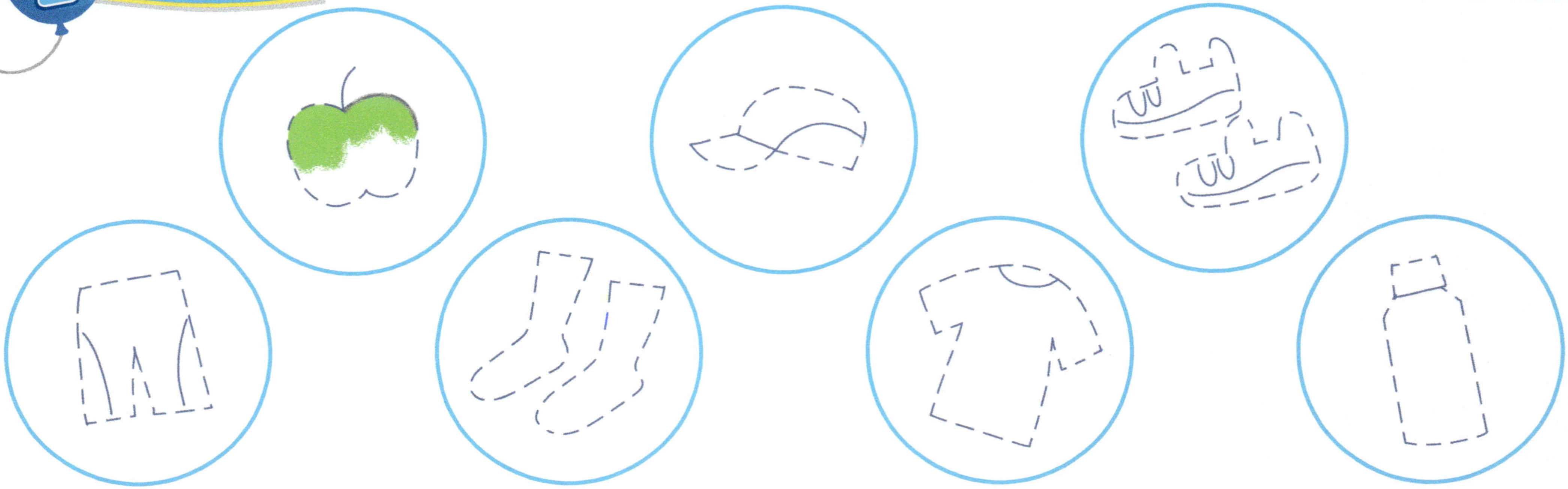

Trace, color and say. Find and circle six differences in the pictures. Point and say. Color the circle on the picture from the story.
Language: apple, hat, shoes, shorts, socks, T-shirt, water

School

A new friend

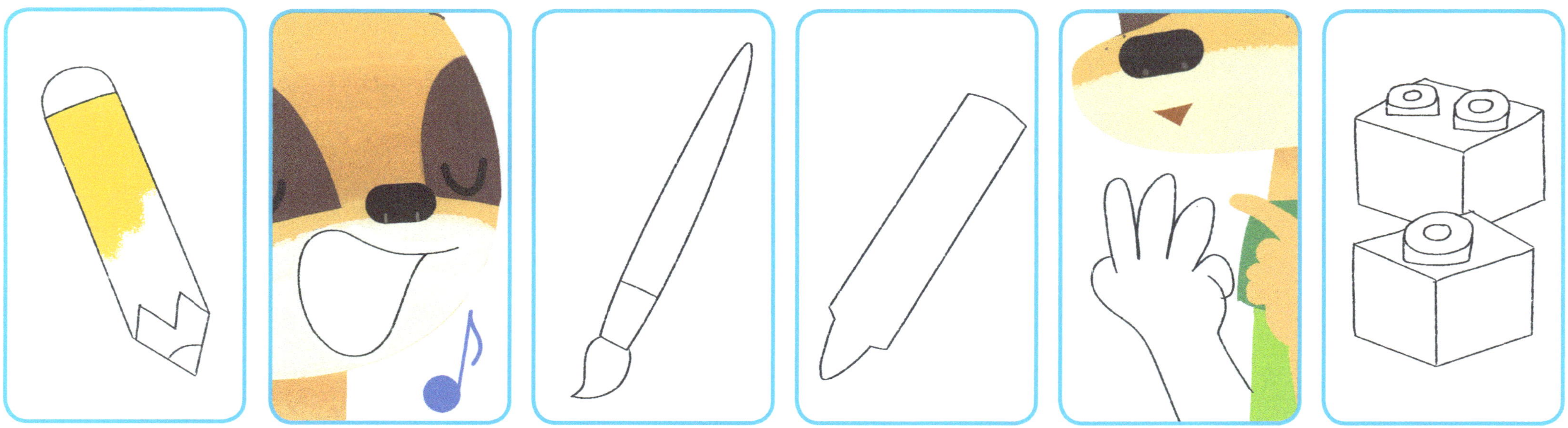

Look and match. Color, point and say.
Language: color, count, draw, paint, play, sing

Circle the activities you do at school. Ask and say.
Language: color, count, dance, draw, jump, paint, play, run, sing, think;
What do you do at school? I (paint) at school.

Find and color Mimi, Dylan, Katy and Leo. Ask and say.

Language: color, count, dance, draw, jump, paint, play, run, sing, think; What do you do at school? I (draw) at school.

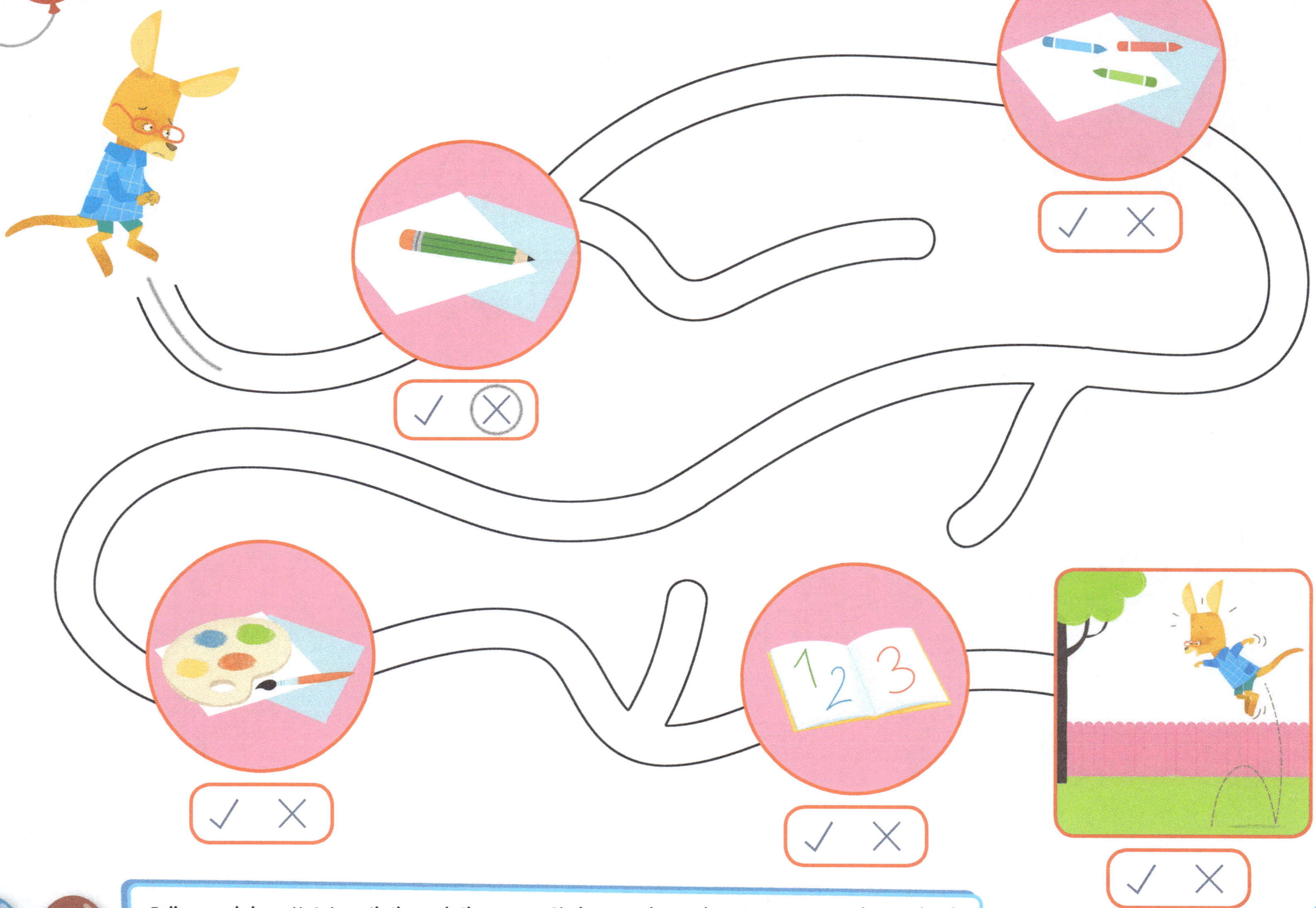

hello

Follow and draw Katy's path through the maze. Circle ✔ to show what Katy wants to do at school. Circle ✘ to show what Katy doesn't want to do at school. Ask and say.

Language: color, count, draw, jump, paint; Do you want to (draw)? No, I don't. I want to (jump).

Imagine it's raining. Draw a picture to show what you want to do. Ask and say. Language: color, dance, draw, paint, play, sing; Do you want to (draw)? Yes, I do / No, I don't. I want to (play). I don't want to (dance).

Values Being kind

Circle the pictures of children being kind at school. Say how you are kind at school.
Language: color, help, play, share, sit down; crayons, friend; I help (my friends).
I share (the crayons).

SOCIAL AND EMOTIONAL LEARNING

Circle the activities you do. Draw and color a picture of you doing exercise. Ask and say.
Language: dance, jump, play soccer, ride my bike, run, swim, walk; What do you do? I (ride my bike).

Match the children doing the same actions. Point and say.

Language: dance, go, shake hands, stand; partner, window

Complete the faces to show what you do at school. Ask and say. Think and circle the number to show your progress. Language: color, count, dance, draw, jump, paint, play, run, sing, think;
What do you do at school? I (draw) at school. Do you want to (sing)? Yes, I do. / No, I don't. I want to (paint).

hello

Project

Find and glue a photo of you doing an activity. Circle the picture of the activity. Ask and say.

Language: dance, draw, paint, play, play soccer, ride my bike, run, sing, swim, walk; What do you do? I (run).

Look and match. Color, point and say.

Language: bench, merry-go-round, pond, seesaw, slide, swing

Find and circle five differences. Point and say.
Language: bench, flowers, grass, merry-go-round, path, pond, seesaw, slide, swings, trees; There's (a pond). There are (trees).

Trace and color what Mimi and Dylan can see in the park. Point and say.

Language: bench, flowers, pond, slide, swings, tree; There's a (bench). There are (flowers).

Story Song

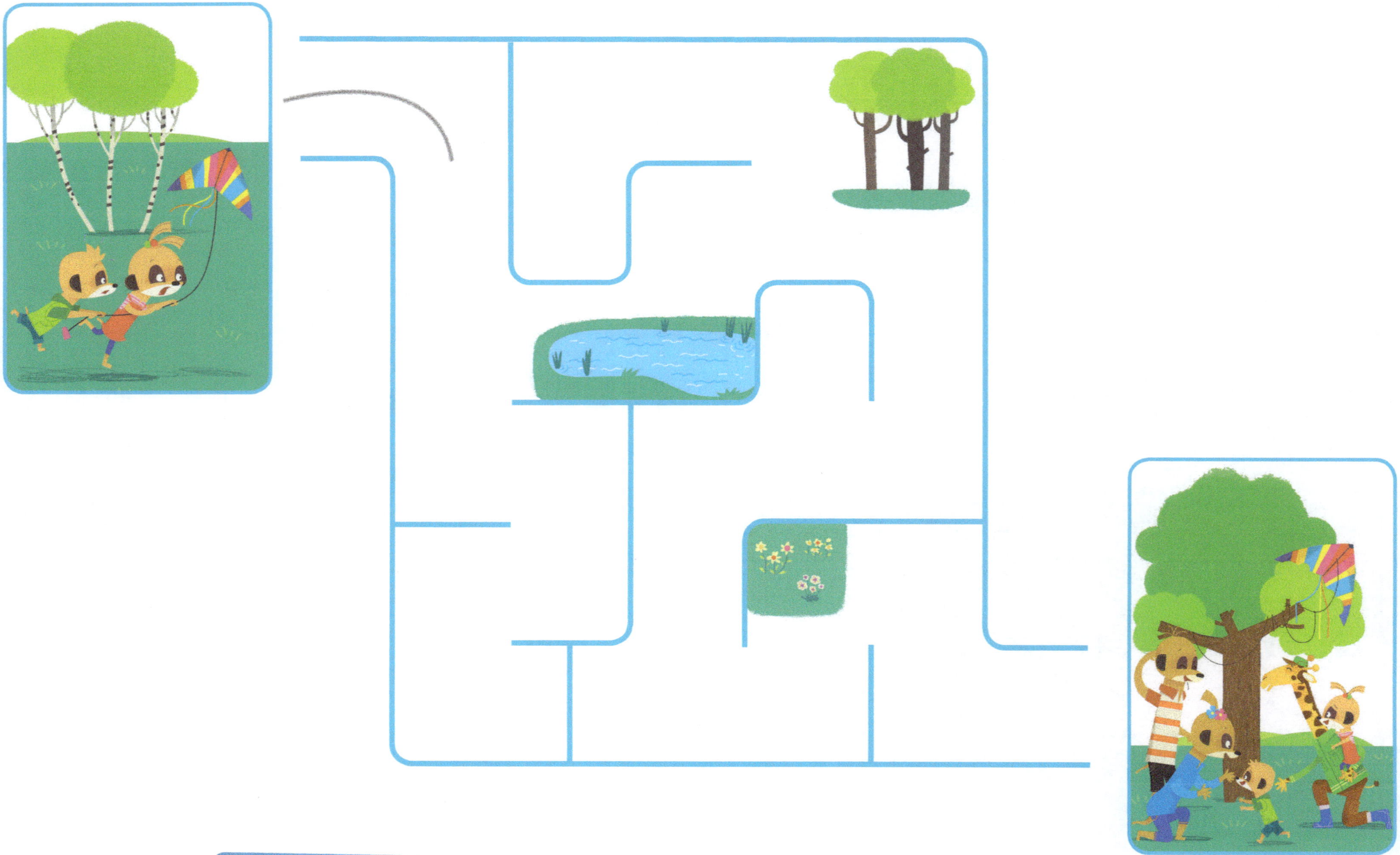

Follow and draw Mimi and Dylan's path through the park maze.
Point and say what Mimi and Dylan see in the park.
Language: flowers, kite, pond, trees; There's the (pond). There are the (trees).

Trace and color what's in the park. Ask and say.
Language: bench, flowers, grass, merry-go-round, path, pond, seesaw, slide, swings, trees; Is there (grass)? Are there (trees)? There's a (bench). There are (swings).

Lesson 6 Values Looking after the environment

Color the pictures of children looking after the environment. Say where you put your trash.
Language: park, trash, trash can; clean; I put my trash in the trash can.

1 2 3 4

Trace the numbers. Match to order the pictures. Draw pictures to show the life cycle of a plant. Point and say. **Language:** flower, leaves, plant, roots, seed, sun, water; numbers; There's a (seed). There are (leaves).

Draw the path from Little Red Riding Hood to Grandma's house. Trace and color. Point and say. Language: apples, cake, cookies, ears, eyes, flowers, house, path, trees, wolf; There are (apples).

Complete the faces to show what you see in the park. Ask and say. Think and circle the number to show your progress. Language: bench, flowers, grass, merry-go-round, path, pond, seesaw, slide, swing, trees; There's a (pond). There are (flowers). Is there a (slide)? Are there (swings)?

Project

The park

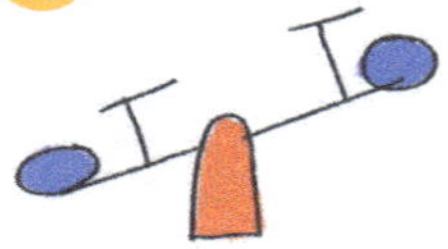

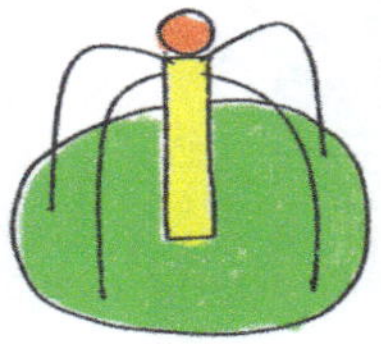

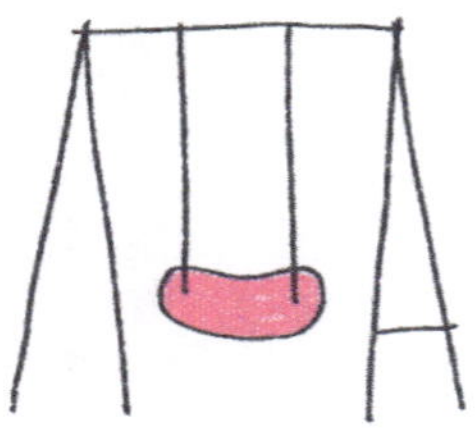
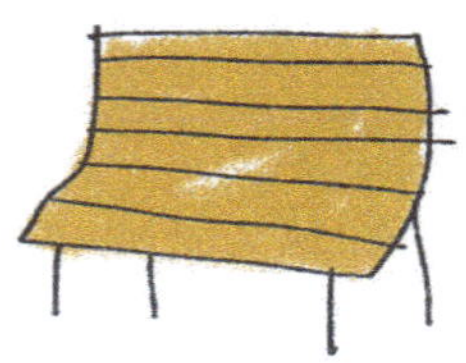

Imagine your favorite park. Draw and paint. Ask and say. Language: bench, flowers, grass, merry-go-round, path, pond, seesaw, slide, swing, trees; There's a (pond). There are (flowers). Is there a (slide)? Are there (swings)? The (flowers) are (yellow). My (swing) is (red). I like the (merry-go-round).

Look and match. Draw and color the missing body parts. Point and say.
Language: crocodile, elephant, hippo, lion, monkey, parrot

Find and circle the wild animals in the picture. Point, ask and say.
Language: crocodile, elephant, giraffe, hippo, lion, monkey, parrot, snake, tiger, zebra; colors; What's that? It's (a snake). It's (green and yellow). It has (big eyes).

1 2 3 4

Number the pictures in order. Circle your favorite picture. Ask and say.
Language: crocodile, lion, monkey, parrot, snake, tiger; colors; numbers 1–4; What's that? It's (a tiger). It has (big eyes). It's (orange and black).

Choose a wild animal costume. Draw and color a picture of you in your costume. Say.
Language: crocodile, lion, monkey, parrot, snake, tiger; I'm a (snake).

hello

Circle the pictures with one wild animal red. Circle the pictures with two or more wild animals green. Ask and say. Language: crocodile, elephant, hippo, monkey, parrot, giraffe; What's that? It's (an elephant). What are those? They're (parrots).

Lesson 6 Values Saying 'thank you'

hello

Check (✓) the pictures to show when you say 'thank you'. Say.
Language: family, friends, teacher; I say 'thank you' to my (friends).

SOCIAL AND EMOTIONAL LEARNING

Match the meerkats. Draw the missing body parts. Color the meerkats. Point and say.
Language: claws, ears, eyes, fur, legs, nose, tail, whiskers; big, small; brown; It has (claws).

1 2 3 4 5

Find and color the monkeys in the picture. Count the monkeys and circle the correct number.
Language: crocodile, monkey; numbers 1–5

Complete the faces to show the wild animals you like. Ask and say. Think and circle the number to show your progress.
Language: crocodile, elephant, giraffe, hippo, lion, monkey, parrot, snake, tiger, zebra; colors; What's that? It's (an elephant). It's (gray). It has (big ears). What are those? They're (hippos).

Project

Find photos and make a collage of wild animals. Circle the wild animals that are in your collage. Ask and say. Language: crocodile, elephant, giraffe, hippo, lion, monkey, parrot, snake, tiger, zebra; colors; What's that? It's (a zebra). It's (black and white). It has (a tail). What are those? They're (snakes).

Daily routines

Giant Joe

Look and match. Trace and color the pictures. Point and say.

Language: brush my hair/teeth, get dressed, get up, wash my face/hands; Mommy, Daddy, Grandma, Grandpa

Follow and draw the paths through the maze. Ask and say.

Language: brush my hair/teeth, get dressed, get up, have breakfast/lunch/dinner, take a shower, wash my face/hands; numbers 1–10; What do you do every day? I (get up).

Color the pictures that show what Mimi and Dylan do before Grandpa tells the story of Giant Joe. Imagine you are Mimi or Dylan. Point and say. Language: brush my hair/teeth, get dressed, get up, have breakfast, wash my face; I (brush my teeth). It's time to (have breakfast).

Story Song

Follow and draw Giant Joe's path through the maze to find Mimi and Dylan. Point and say.
Language: brush my hair/teeth, get dressed, get up, have breakfast/dinner, wash my face/hands; I'm a giant. My name is Joe. I (get up).

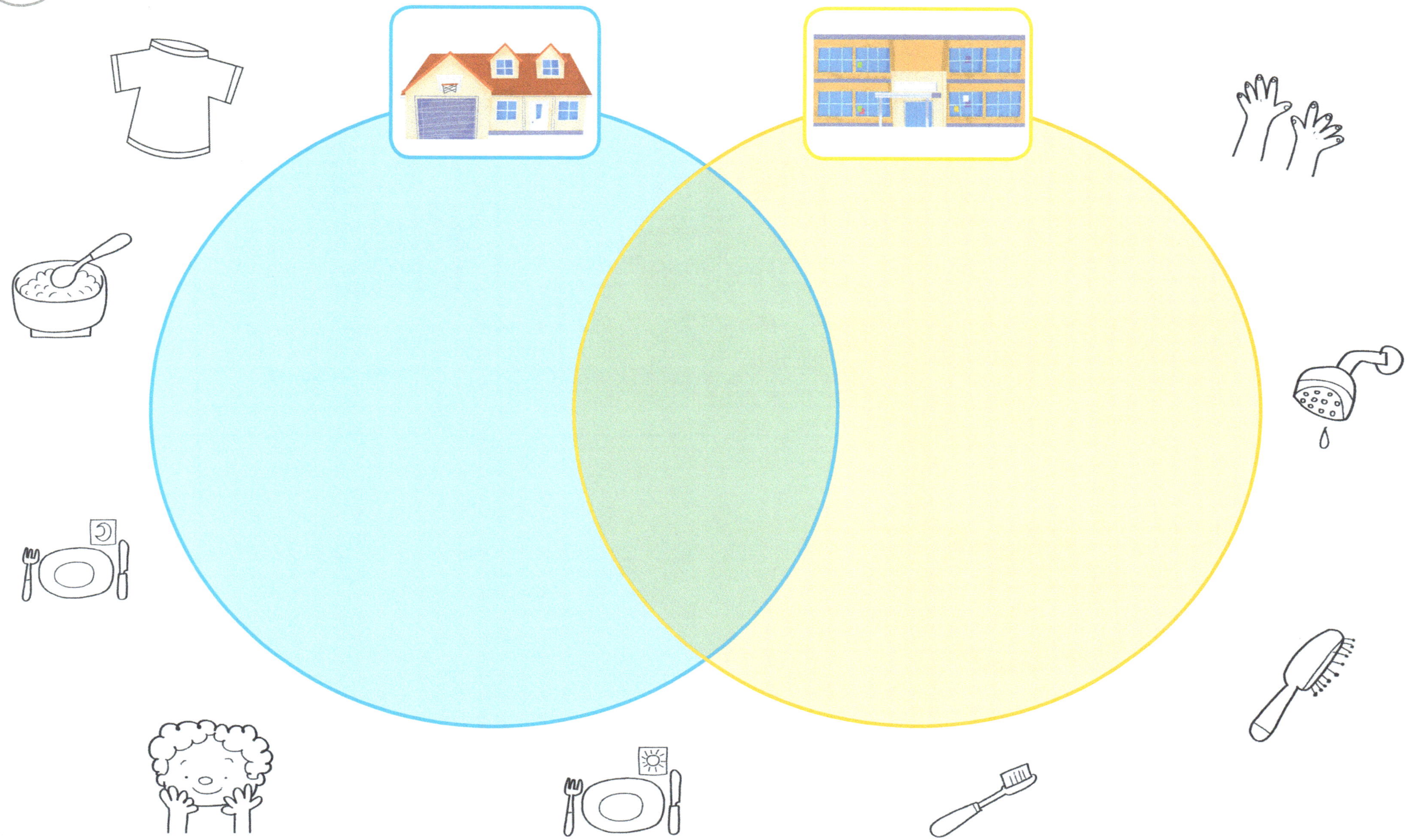

Draw your daily routines in the correct part of the diagram for you. Ask and say. Language: brush my hair/teeth, get dressed, have breakfast/lunch/dinner, take a shower, wash my face/hands; home, school; What do you do at (home)? I (have breakfast) at home. I don't (take a shower) at school. Do you (have lunch) at school? Yes, I do. / No, I don't.

Draw and color pictures of two of your daily routines. Point and say.
Language: eat, learn, play, sleep; I (play) every day.

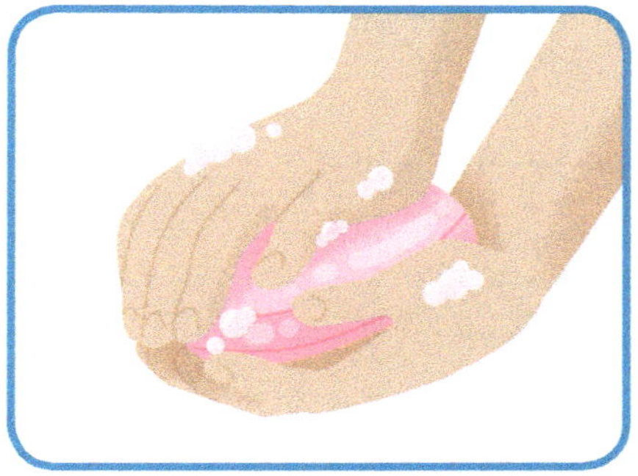

Make a hand print with paint. Talk about the colors. Wash your hands. Point and say.
Language: faucet, hands, soap, towel, water; colors; My hand is (blue and yellow).
I (wash my hands) with (soap).

Match the bowls, chairs and beds to the bears. Color Daddy Bear's things red, Mommy Bear's things green, and Baby Bear's things blue. Point and say. Language: bed, bowl, chair; big, small, tiny; Mommy, Daddy, Baby Bear; This (bowl) is (small).

Complete the faces to show your daily routines. Ask and say. Think and circle the number to show your progress.

Language: brush my hair/teeth, get dressed, get up, have breakfast/lunch/dinner, take a shower, wash my face/hands; What do you do every day? I (get up). I don't (have dinner) at (school). Do you (have lunch) at (home)? Yes, I do. / No, I don't.

Project

Make a daily routine wheel. Draw and color pictures to show what you do every day. Ask and say.

Language: brush my hair/teeth, get dressed, get up, have breakfast/lunch/dinner, take a shower, wash my face/hands; What do you do every day? I (have breakfast). I don't (take a shower). Do you (wash your face)? Yes, I do. / No, I don't.

Meals

Toast, toast, toast!

Look and match. Trace and color the food. Point and say.
Language: chicken, pancake, rice, salad, toast, yogurt

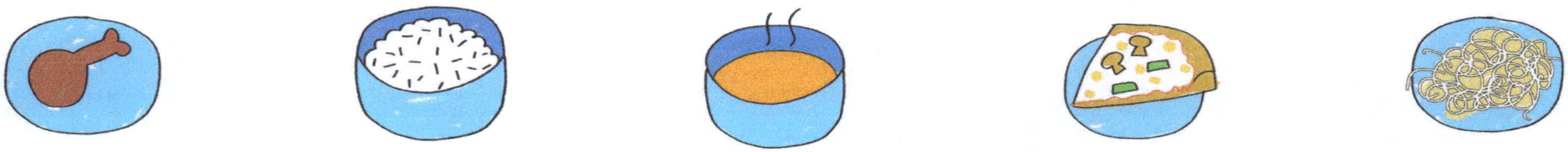

Draw food you have for breakfast, lunch and dinner. Ask and say.
Language: chicken, fish, pancakes, pizza, rice, salad, soup, spaghetti, toast, yogurt; breakfast, lunch, dinner; What do you have for (breakfast)? I have (pancakes). What about you?

Draw pictures to show what Dylan and Mimi want for breakfast, lunch and dinner in the story. Ask and say. Language: chicken, fish, pancakes, pizza, rice, salad, soup, spaghetti, toast, yogurt; breakfast, lunch, dinner; Do you want (pancakes)? No, thank you. I want (toast).

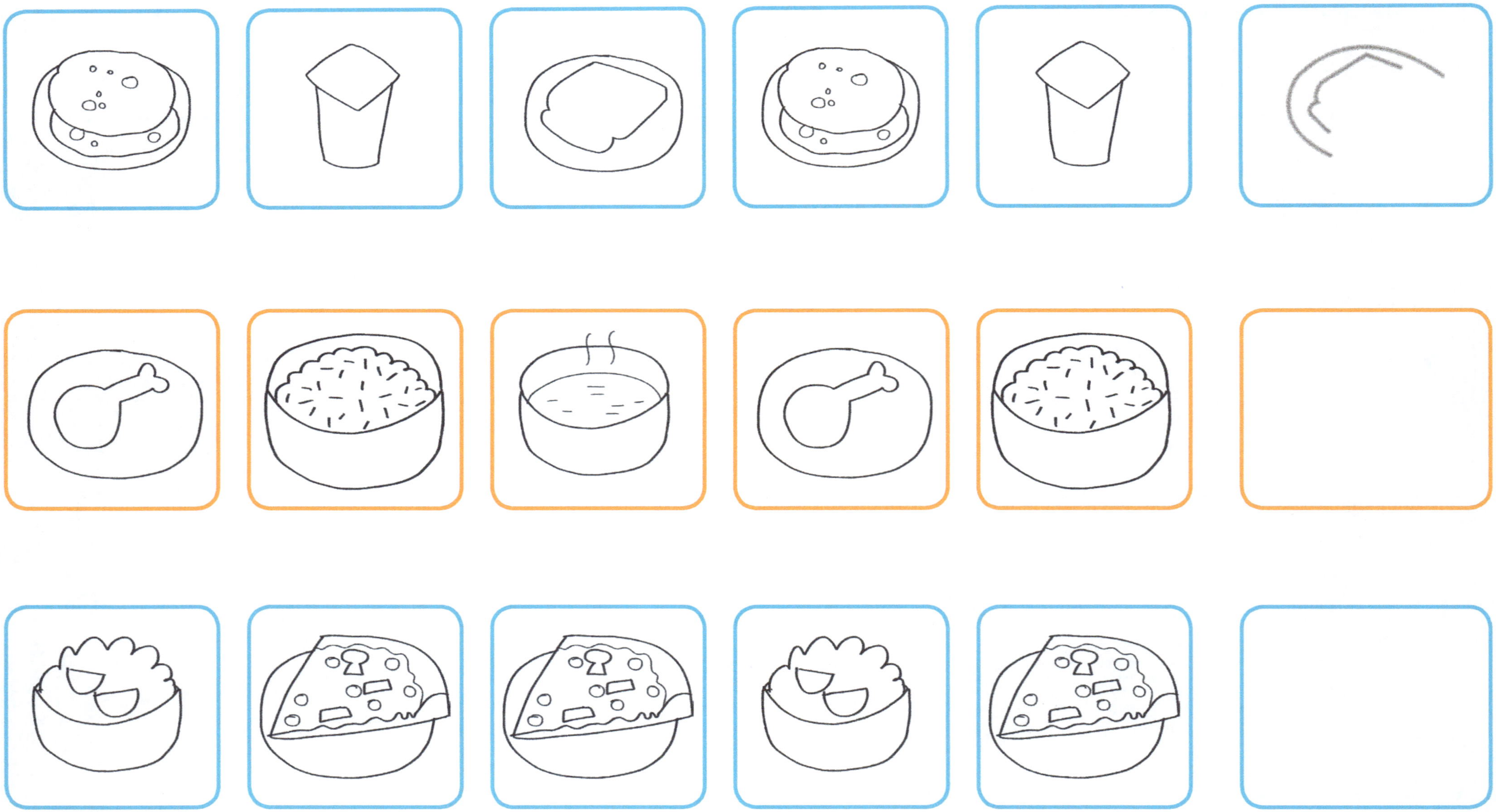

Draw the next food in the sequence. Color the food Mimi wants. Ask and say.
Language: chicken, pancakes, pizza, rice, salad, soup, toast, yogurt; Do you want (chicken)? Yes, please. / No, thank you. I want (toast). I like (toast).

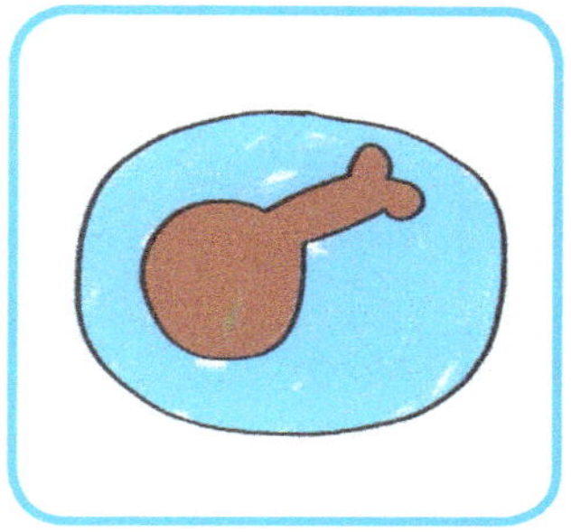

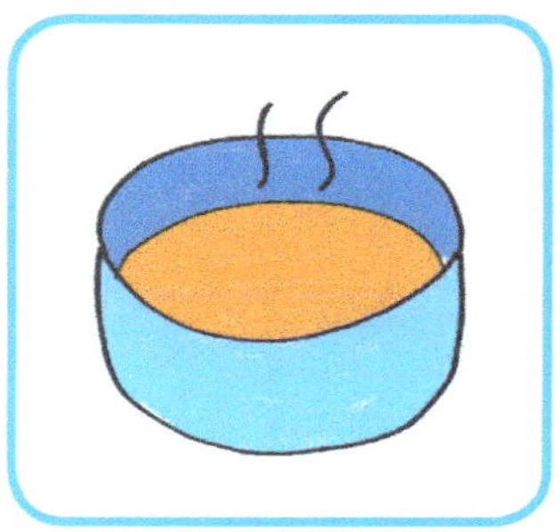

Draw food you want and don't want for lunch. Ask and say.

Language: chicken, fish, pizza, rice, salad, soup; What do you want for lunch? I want (chicken). I don't want (fish). Do you want (soup)? Yes, please. / No, thank you.

1 2 3 4

1

Number the pictures in order. Draw and color the food in the story. Ask and say.
Language: carrots, food, peas, soup, tomatoes; green, orange, red; numbers 1–4; Do you want (peas)? Yes, please. / No, thank you. I like (soup). I don't like (orange) food.

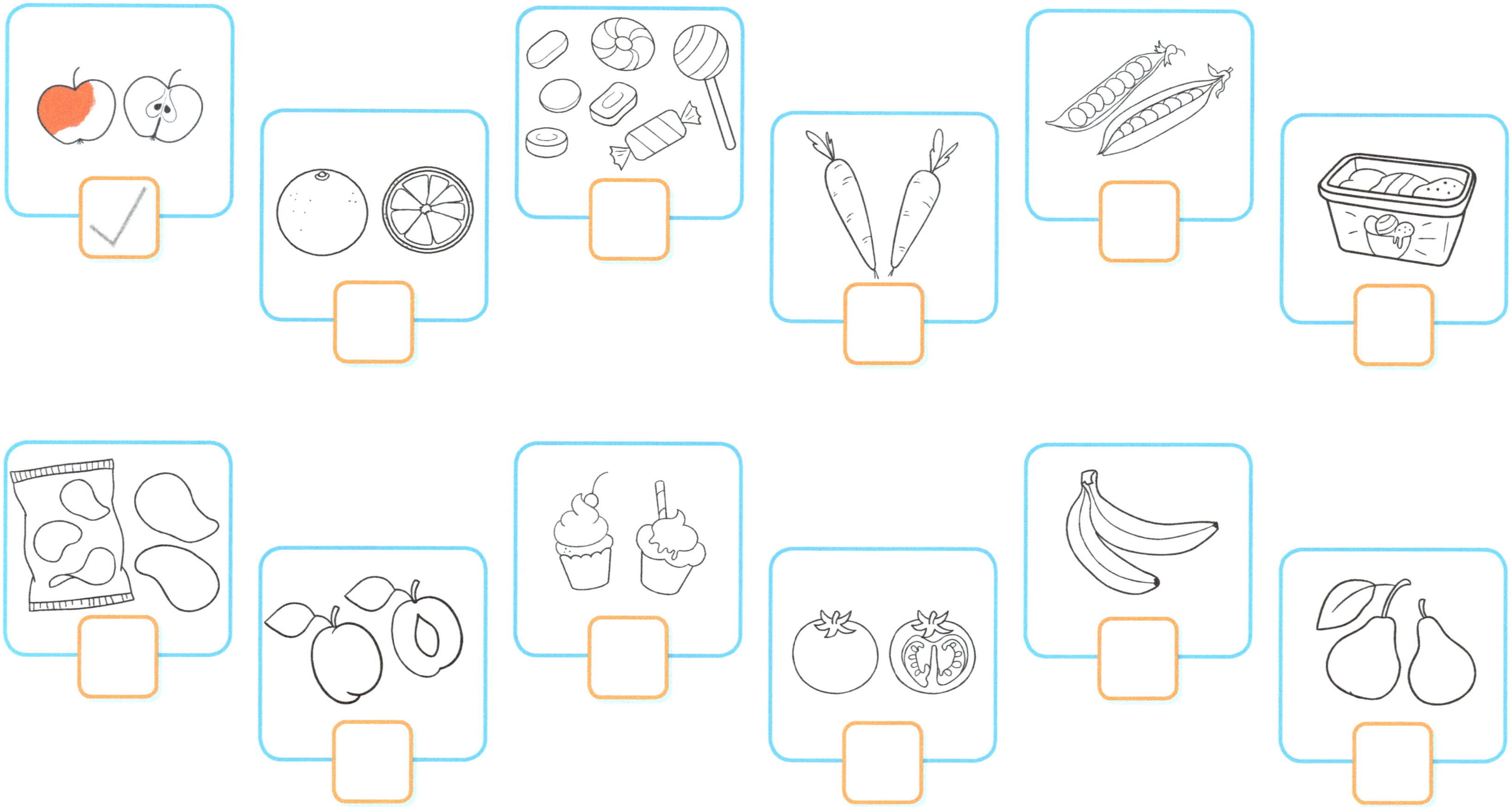

Check (✔) and color the food that is good for you. Point and say.

Language: apples, bananas, candy, carrots, chips, cupcakes, ice cream, oranges, pears, peas, plums, tomatoes; (Oranges) (are) good for you.

1 5 10

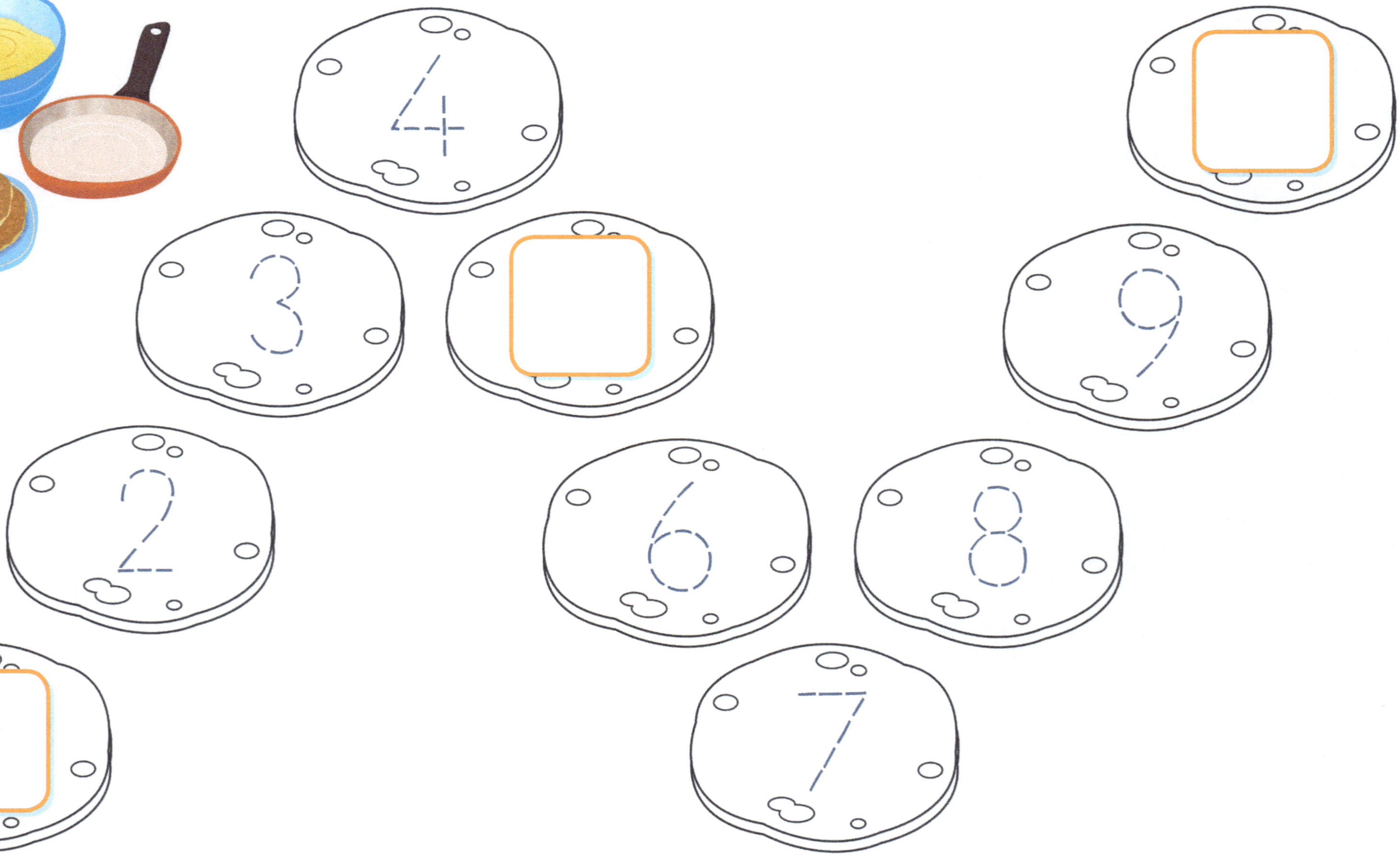

Write the numbers on pancakes 1, 5 and 10. Trace the numbers on the other pancakes. Point and say the numbers.

Language: pancakes; numbers 1–10

Complete the faces to show the food you have for breakfast, lunch or dinner. Ask and say. Think and circle the number to show your progress. Language: chicken, fish, pancake, pizza, rice, salad, soup, spaghetti, toast, yogurt; breakfast, lunch, dinner; What do you have for (breakfast)? I have (yogurt). What do you want for (lunch)? I want (toast). I don't want (pizza). Do you want (salad)?

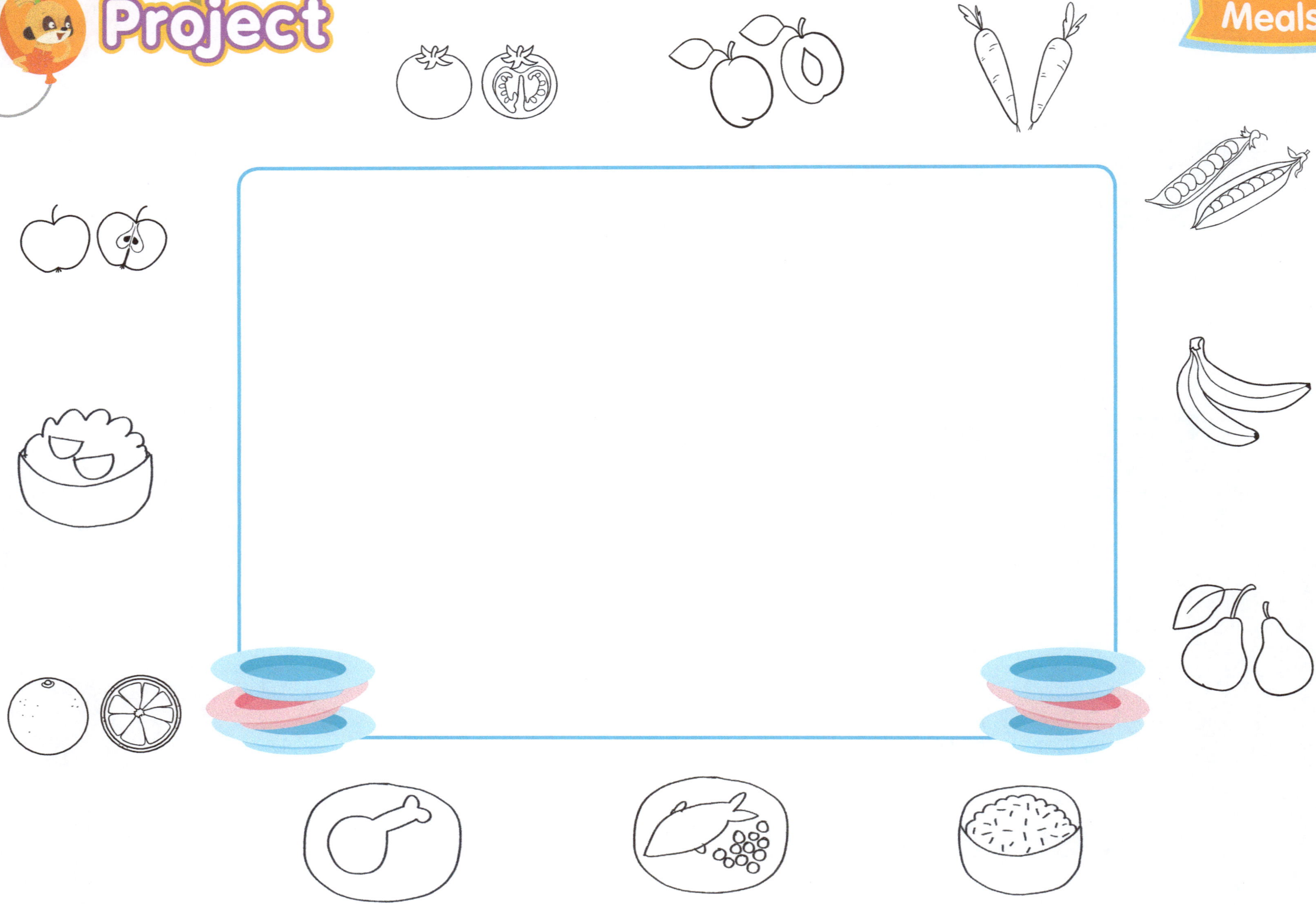

Find photos and make a collage of food that is good for you. Circle and color the food in your collage. Point and say. Language: apples, bananas, carrots, chicken, fish, oranges, pears, peas, plums, rice, salad, tomatoes; (Fish) is good for you. (Apples) are good for you.

Town
A day out

Follow and draw the path through the town maze. Trace and color Mimi and Dylan's house. Point and say. Language: mall, movie theater, museum, swimming pool, toy store, zoo

Choose and draw a place you want to go and a place you don't want to go. Ask and say.
Language: bookstore, mall, movie theater, museum, park, restaurant, supermarket, swimming pool, toy store, zoo; Do you want to go to the (bookstore)? Yes, please. / No, thanks.

Trace the ✓ or ✗ to show where Mimi and Dylan go or don't go in the story. Ask and say. Language: bookstore, mall, movie theater, museum, park, restaurant, supermarket, swimming pool, toy store, zoo; dinosaur, space; Do you want to go to the (dinosaur museum)? Yes, I do. / No, I don't. I want to go to the (space museum). Let's go to the (mall).

Lesson 4

Story Song

Trace and color the movie *Dinosaurs in space*. Say.

Language: dinosaurs, movie theater, space; I want to learn about (space).

Plan your visit to the museum. Draw a line to show your route. Write numbers to show the order.

Ask and say. Language: dinosaur, fish, planet; museum; numbers 1–3; Do you want to see the (dinosaurs)? No, thank you. Where do you want to go? I want to go to (a museum). I want to see the (planets).

Values Interest in learning

Trace the pictures of children learning. Choose and color a picture that shows how you like to learn. Say. **Language:** ask questions, find out about my world, look at books, play games, talk to friends, watch movies/TV; I want to learn. Do you? I (look at books). I (play games).

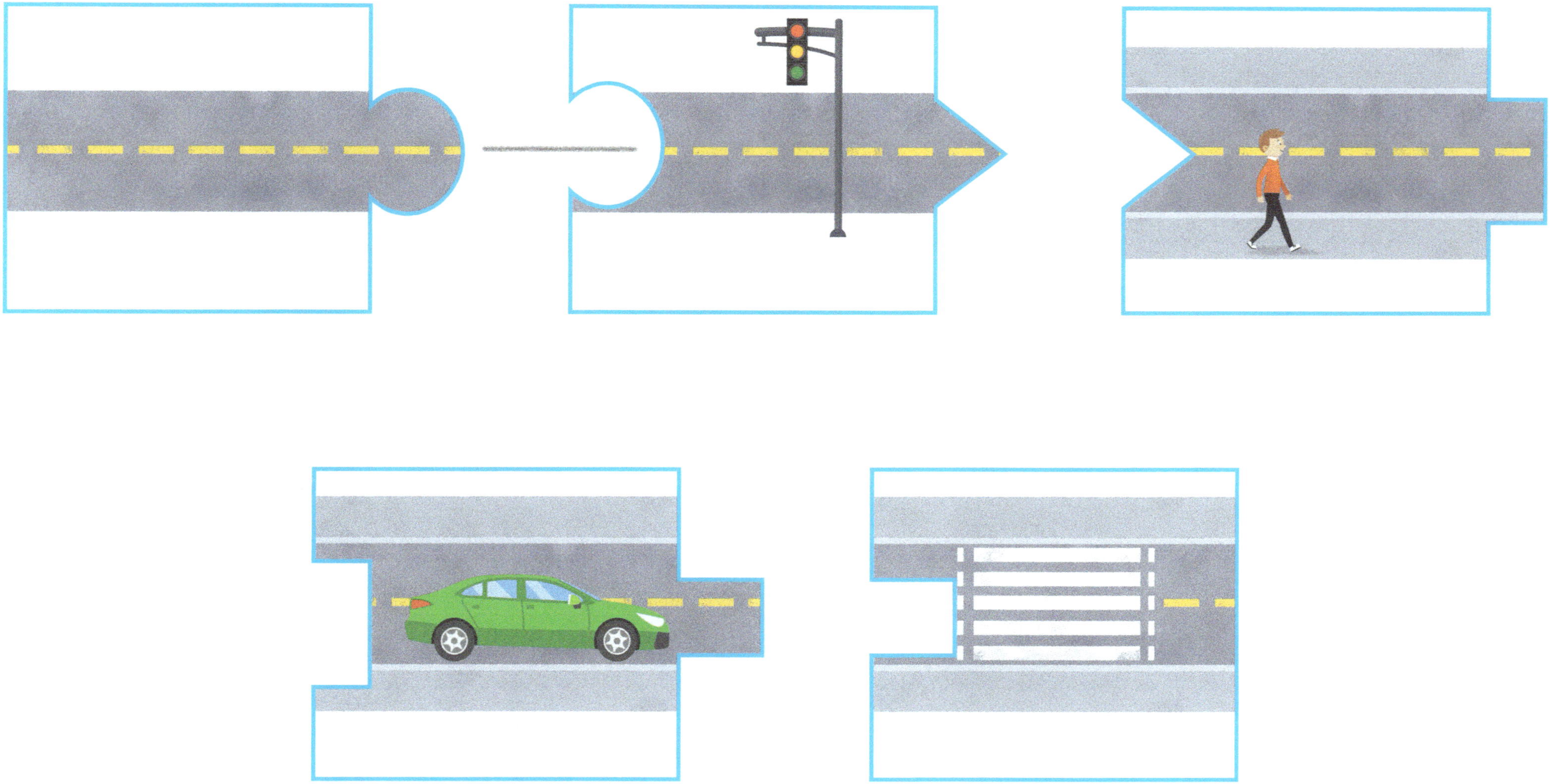

Connect the puzzle pieces. Point and say. Circle the car green. Circle the stoplights red.
Language: car, crosswalk, sidewalk, stoplights, street

Connect the dots to complete the picture. Color the enormous carrot. Point and say.
Language: carrot; boy, girl, man, woman; pull; numbers 1–10; The (man) pulls the (woman).

Complete the faces to show places you want to go to in your town. Ask and say. Think and circle the number to show your progress. Language: bookstore, mall, movie theater, museum, park, restaurant, supermarket, swimming pool, toy store, zoo; Do you want to go to (the zoo)? Yes, I do. / No, I don't. Where do you want to go? I want/don't want to go to (the park).

Project

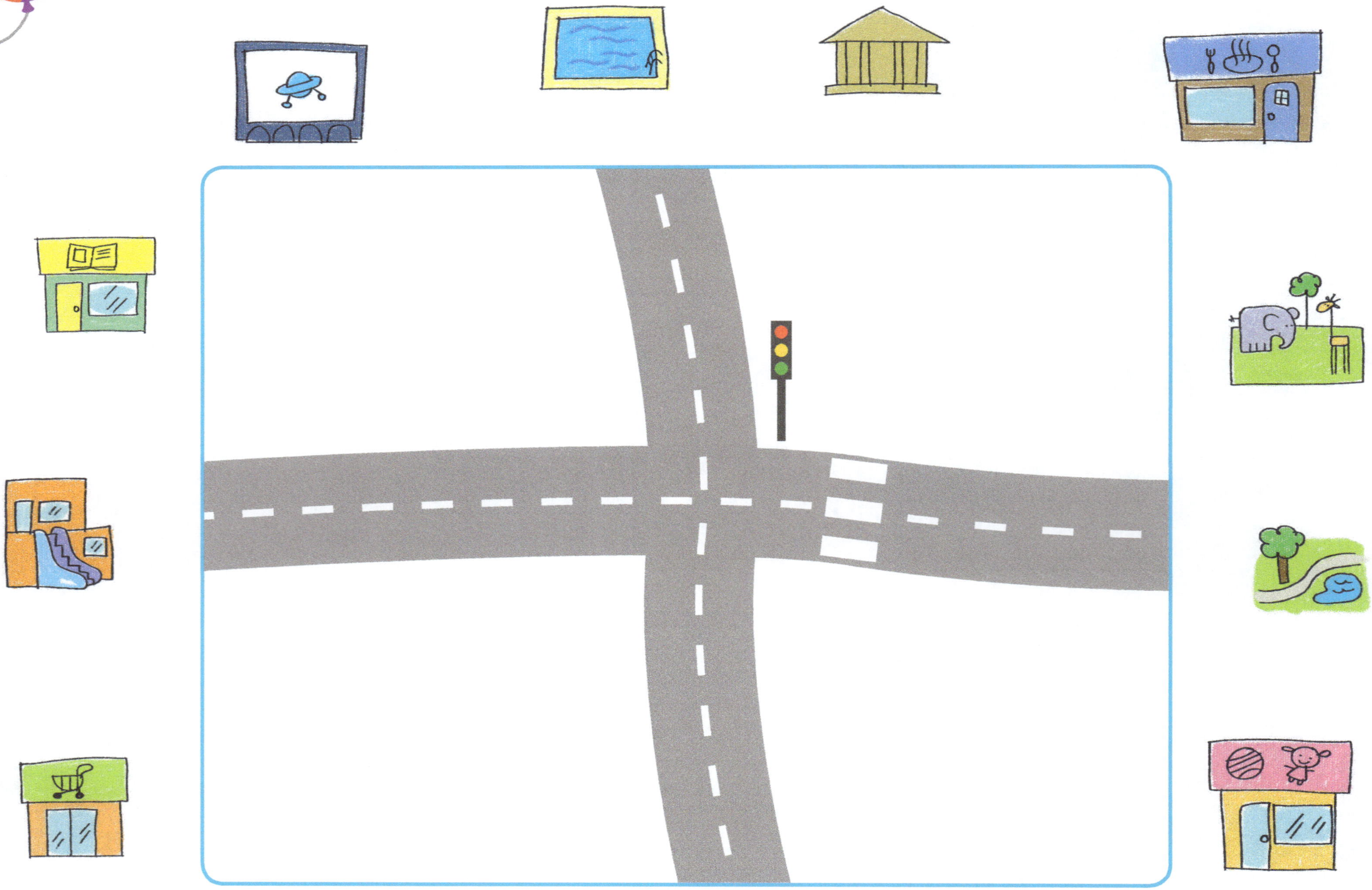

Design a town. Choose and draw four places in your town. Ask and say. **Language:** bookstore, mall, movie theater, museum, park, restaurant, supermarket, swimming pool, toy store, zoo; Where do you want to go? I want to go to the (supermarket). I don't want to go to the (mall). Do you want to go to the (zoo)? Yes, I do. / No, I don't. I like the (park). Do you like the (toy store)? Yes, I do. / No, I don't.

Draw the next musical instrument in the sequence. Point and say.

Language: drum, guitar, maracas, piano, recorder, tambourine

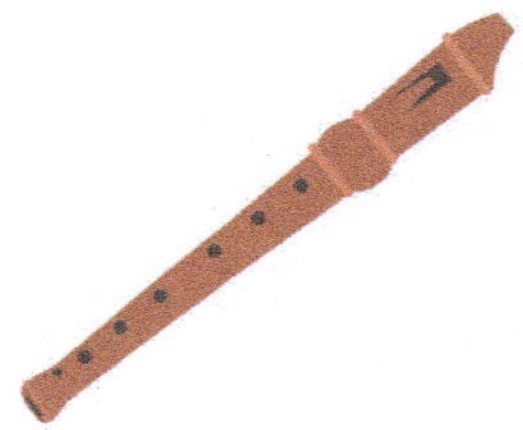

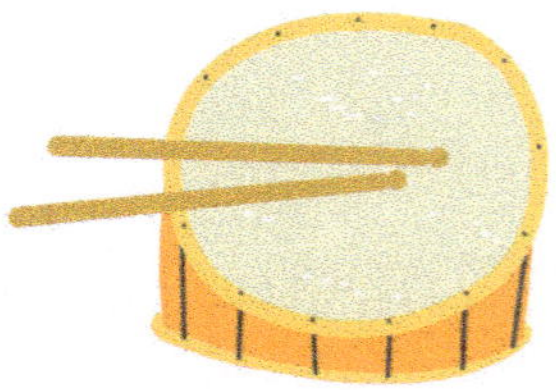

Circle your favorite music activity. Draw a picture of you doing it. Ask and say.
Language: drum, guitar, maracas, piano, recorder, tambourine; clap, dance, listen, sing;
What are you doing? I'm (playing the drum). I'm (clapping).

Trace the musical instruments. Match them to the characters who play them in the class show in the story. Point and say.

Language: drum, maracas, recorder, tambourine; I'm playing the (recorder).

Choose and circle an instrument. Draw a picture of you playing the instrument in the class show. Point and say. Language: drum, guitar, maracas, piano, recorder, tambourine; I'm playing the (drum).

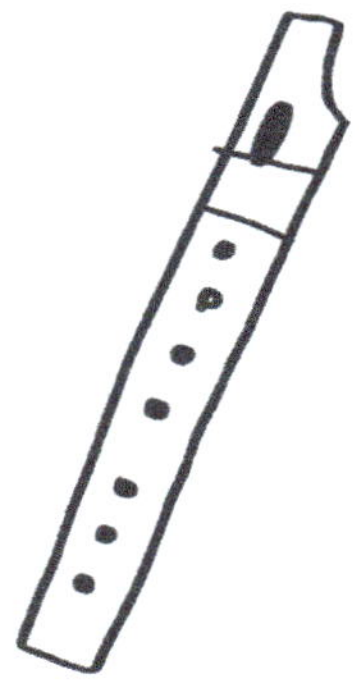

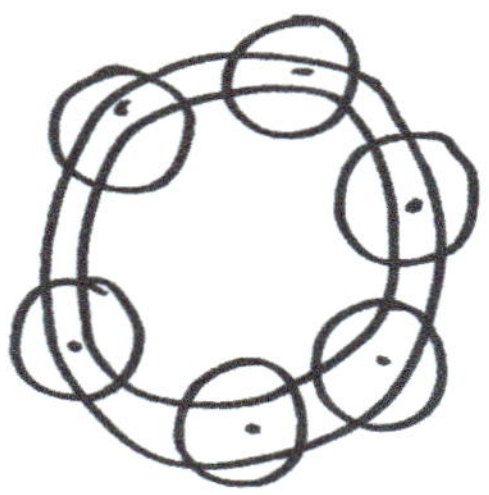
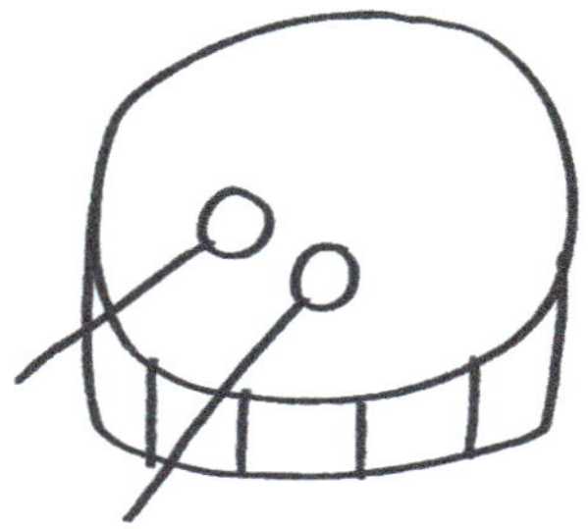

Color the musical instruments you like playing. Ask and say.
Language: drum, guitar, maracas, piano, recorder, tambourine;
Do you like playing the (piano)? Yes, I do. / No, I don't. I like playing the (recorder).

Draw a picture of you practicing something. Ask and say.
Language: dance, draw, play the recorder, read, ride a bike, sing; What are you doing? I'm (singing). I'm practicing.

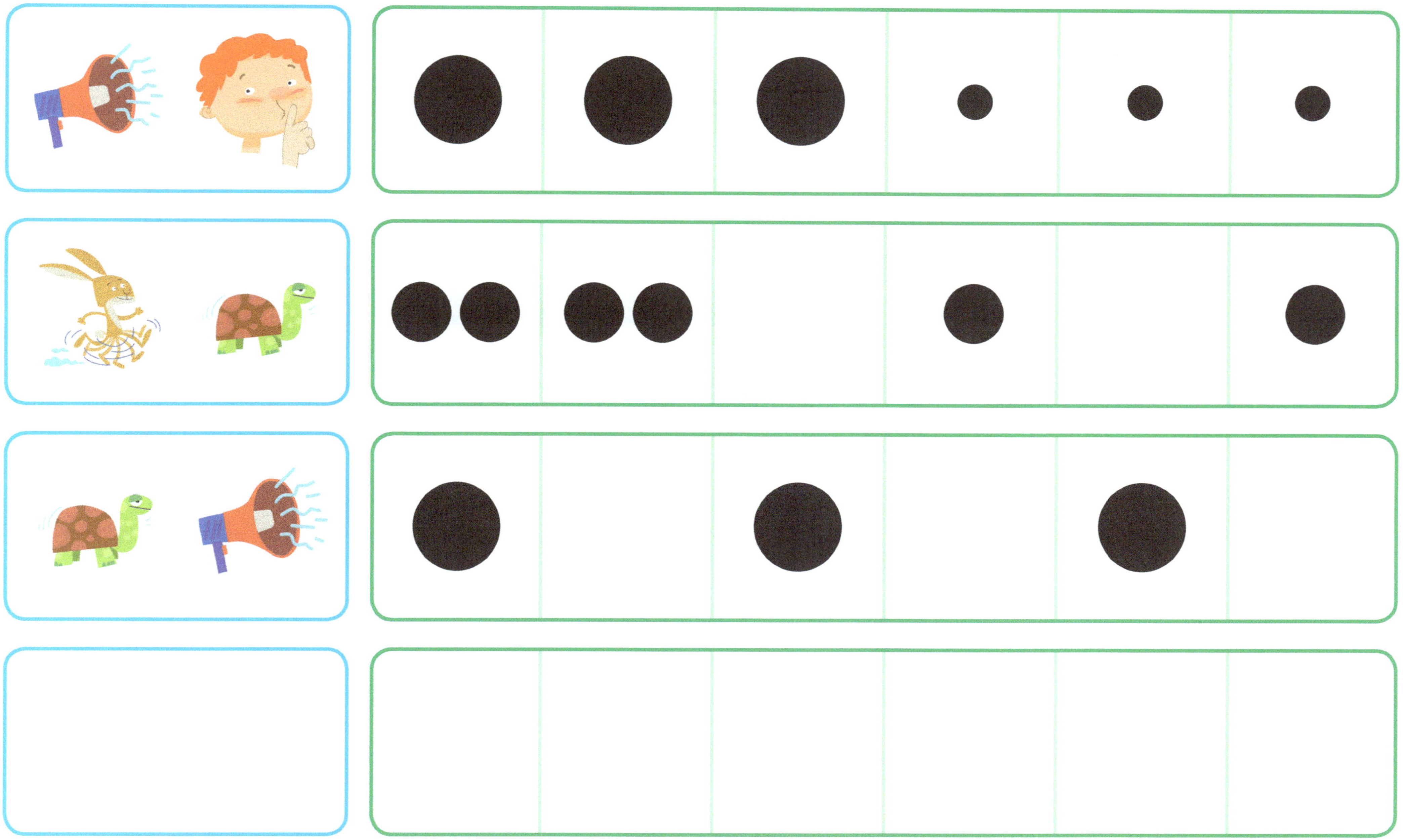

Look and clap the three rhythms. Think of another rhythm. Draw pictures and circles to show the rhythm. Clap and say.
Language: fast, slow, loud, quiet; It's (slow and loud).

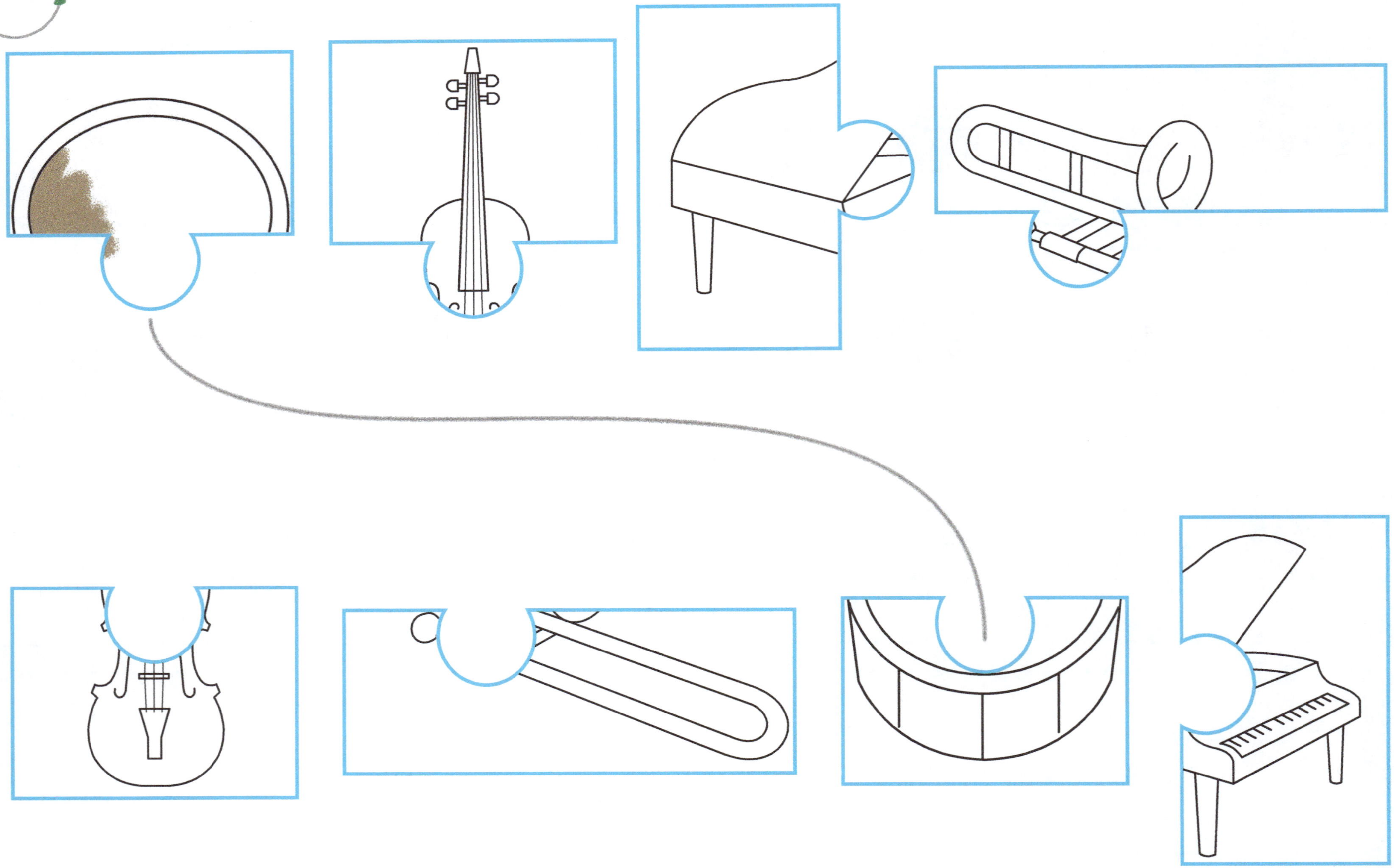

Match and color the musical instruments from *I am the music man*. Point and say.
Language: drum, piano, trombone, violin; What can you play? I play the (violin).

Complete the faces to show the musical instruments and activities you like. Ask and say. Think and circle the number to show your progress. **Language:** drum, guitar, maracas, piano, recorder, tambourine; clap, dance, listen, sing; What are you doing? I'm playing the (recorder). I'm (singing). Do you like playing the (drum)? Yes, I do. / No, I don't. I like playing the (guitar).

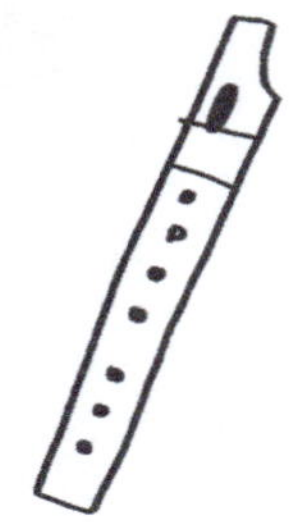

Find photos and make a collage of musical instruments. Circle and color the instruments in your collage. Point and say. Language: drum, guitar, maracas, piano, recorder, tambourine; My (drum) is (red and blue).

Bugs
Honey for dinner

Find and circle the bugs. Point and say. Color.
Language: ant, bee, butterfly, ladybug, snail, worm

Look and match. Draw and color what's missing from each bug. Ask and say.

Language: ant, bee, butterfly, ladybug, snail, worm; legs, spots, stripes, wings;
Does (a bee) have (legs)? Yes, it does. / No, it doesn't.

1 2 3 4

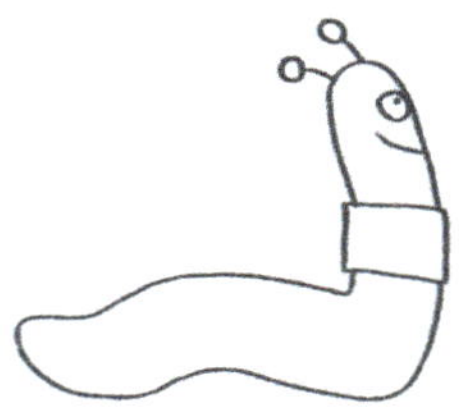

Number the pictures in order. Color your favorite bug from the story. Ask and say.
Language: butterfly, ladybug, snail, worm; legs, spots, stripes, wings; colors; numbers 1–4; A (ladybug) is (red and black). It has (spots). Does it have (legs)? Yes, it does. / No, it doesn't.

Circle the character who is with the bees in *We want to get some honey*.
Point, ask and say. Draw and color more bees.
Language: bee, butterfly, ladybug, snail, worm; Where are the (bees)? Here are the (bees).

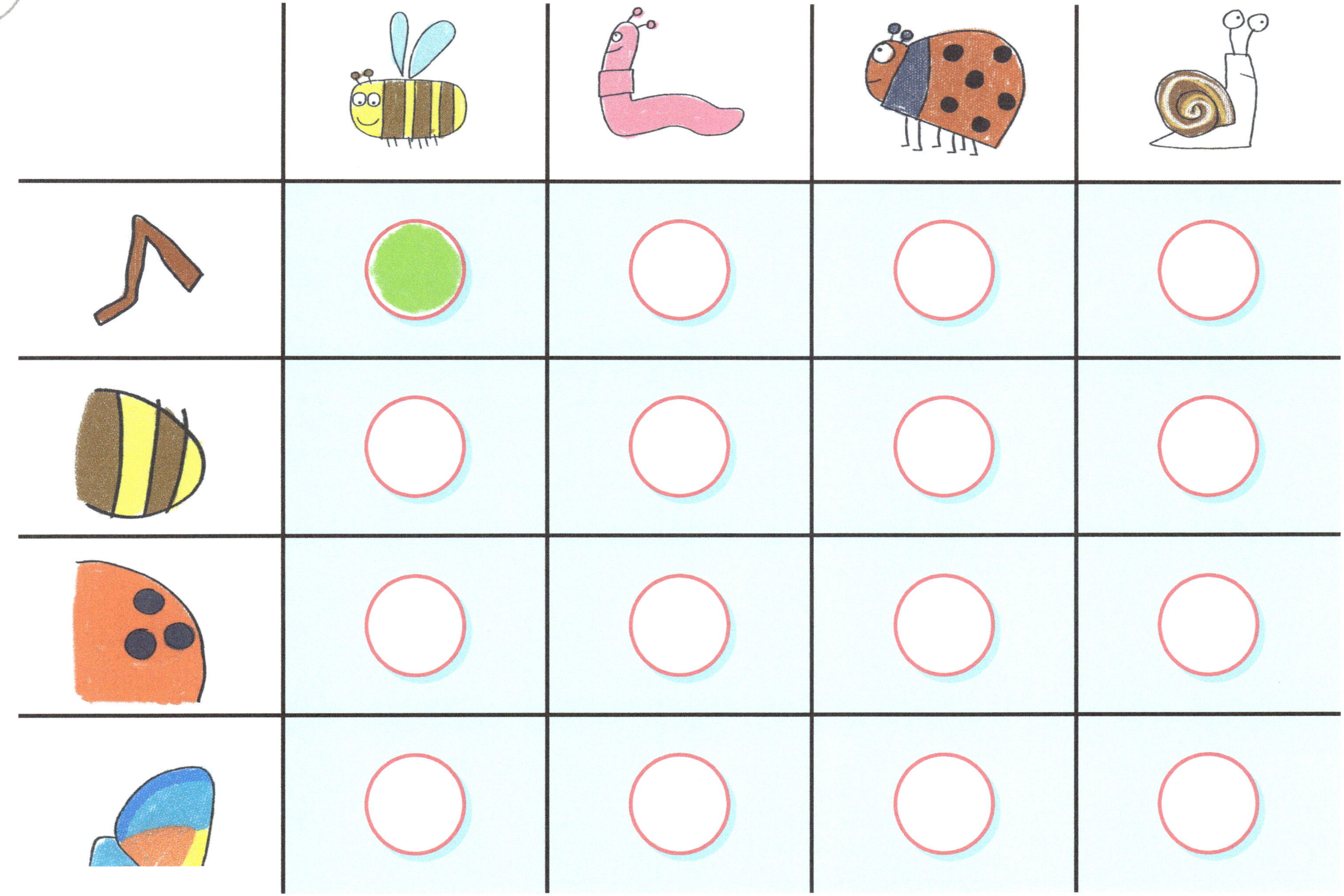

Color the circles green to show what each bug has. Color the circles red to show what each bug doesn't have. Ask and say. Language: bee, ladybug, snail, worm; legs, spots, stripes, wings; Does it have (legs)? Yes, it does. / No, it doesn't. It has (wings). It doesn't have (stripes).

Values Caring for our world

Color the pictures to show what you care for. Point and say.

Language: animals, bugs, family, flowers, friends, nature, trees; I care for (nature).

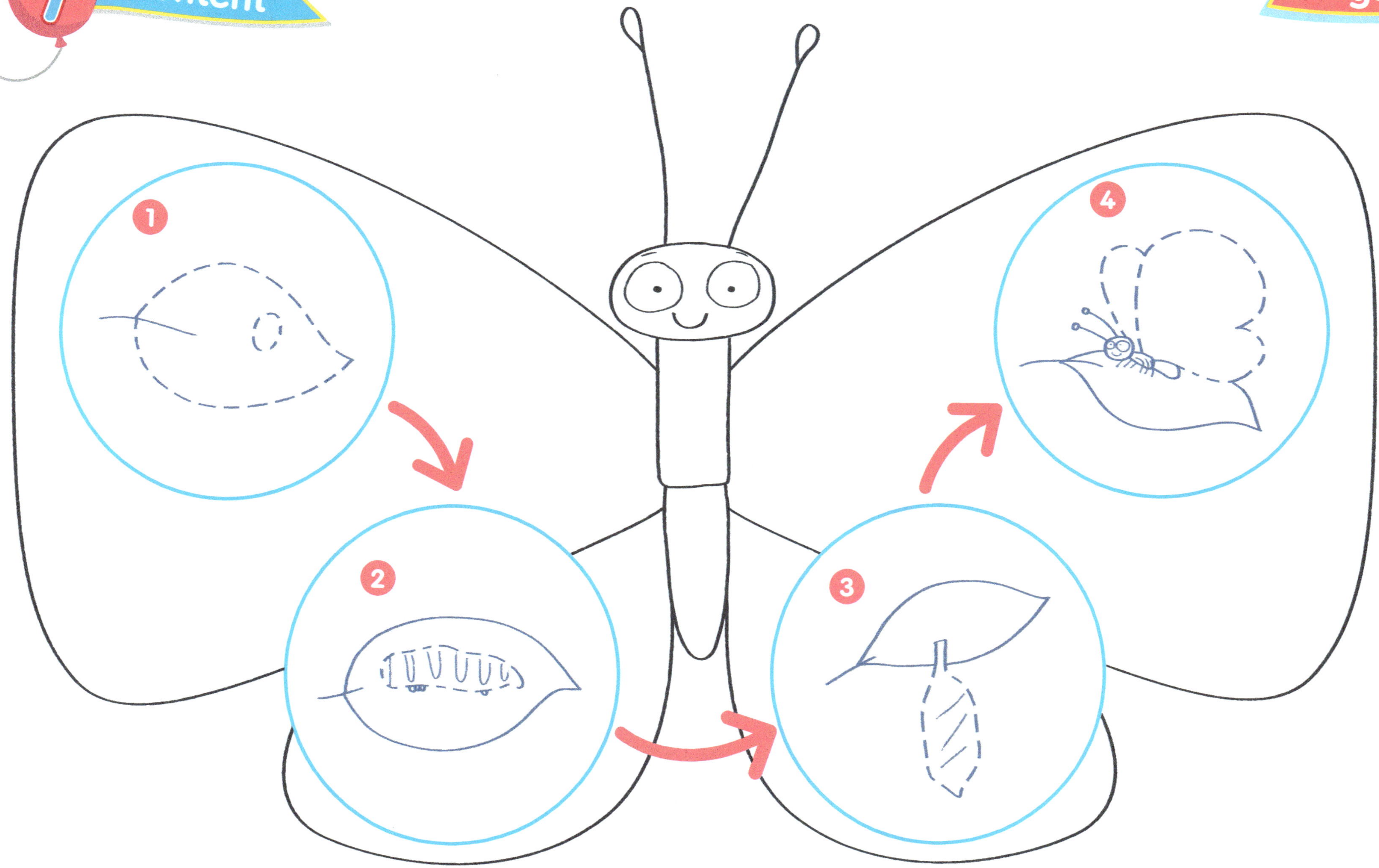

Trace and color the life cycle of the butterfly. Point and say.

Language: butterfly, caterpillar, chrysalis, egg, leaf; numbers 1–4; It's (an egg) on a (leaf).

Color the circle on the picture of summer green. Color the circle on the picture of winter blue. Color the character who collects food. Point and say. Language: ant, food, grasshopper; happy, hungry, sad; summer, winter; It's (summer). The grasshopper is (happy).

Complete the faces to show the bugs you like and what they have. Ask and say. Think and circle the number to show your progress. Language: ant, bee, butterfly, ladybug, snail, worm; legs, spots, stripes, wings; Does it have (spots)? Yes, it does. / No, it doesn't. It has (stripes). It doesn't have (wings).

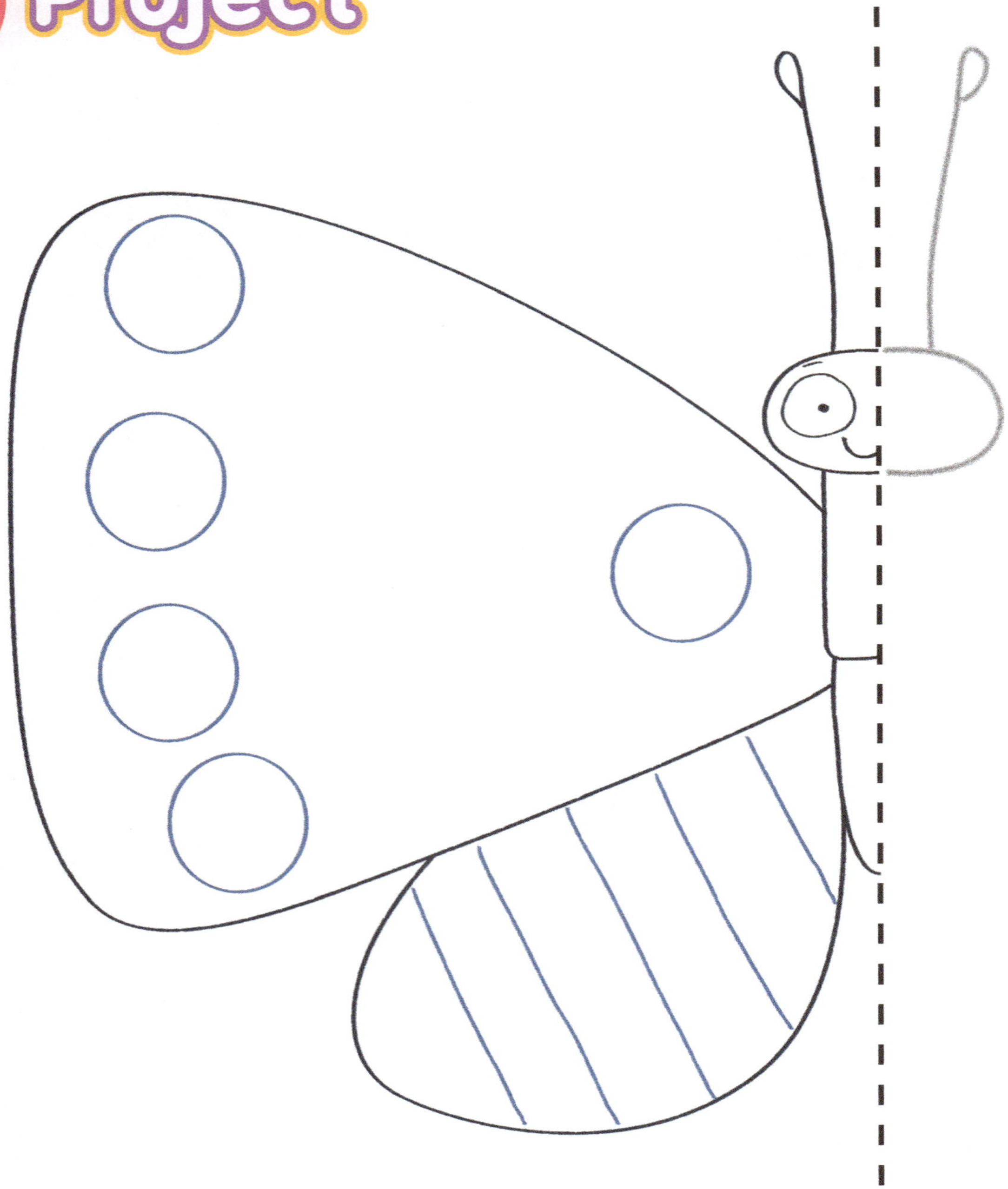

Draw the other half of the butterfly. Color your butterfly so both sides are the same. Ask and say.
Language: butterfly; spots, stripes, wings; colors; Does it have (wings)? Yes, it does. / No, it doesn't.
It has/doesn't have (stripes). My butterfly is (red, blue and yellow).

Colors

Match the animals. Use the key to color the animals in the picture. Point and say.
Language: black, blue, gray, red, white, yellow; It's (blue).

Colors

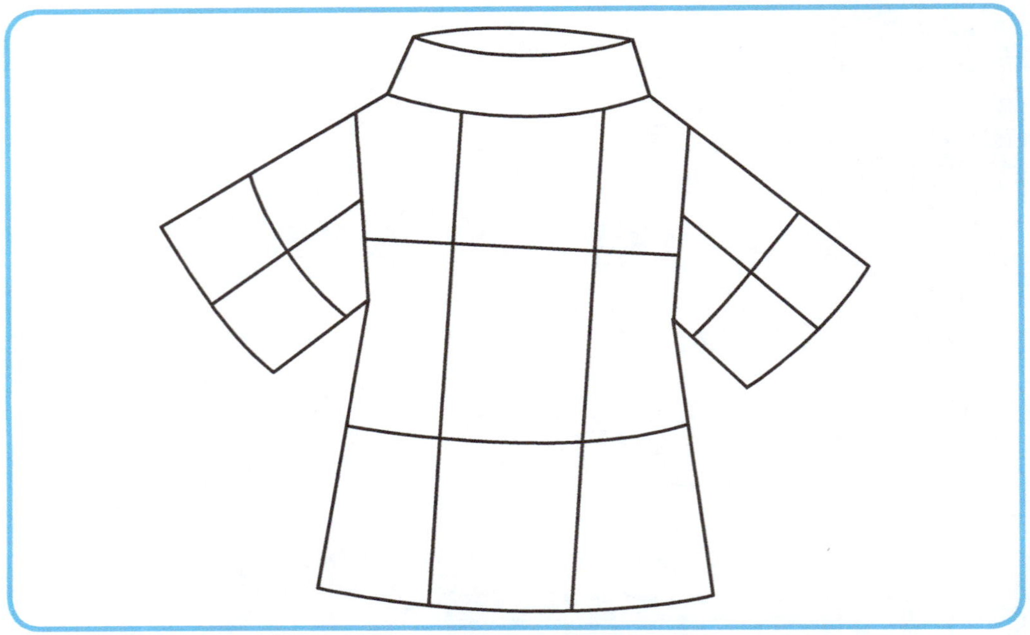

Choose and color a T-shirt for you and a friend. Point and say.
Language: brown, gray, green, orange, pink, purple; It's (orange).

Numbers 10 20 30 40 50 60 70 80 90 100

10 20 30 40 50 60 70 80 90 100

Count and circle groups of ten stars. Count the groups of stars. Circle the total number of stars. Point and say. Language: stars; numbers 10–100; I can see (fifty) stars.

Numbers 5 10 15 20 25 30 35 40 45 50

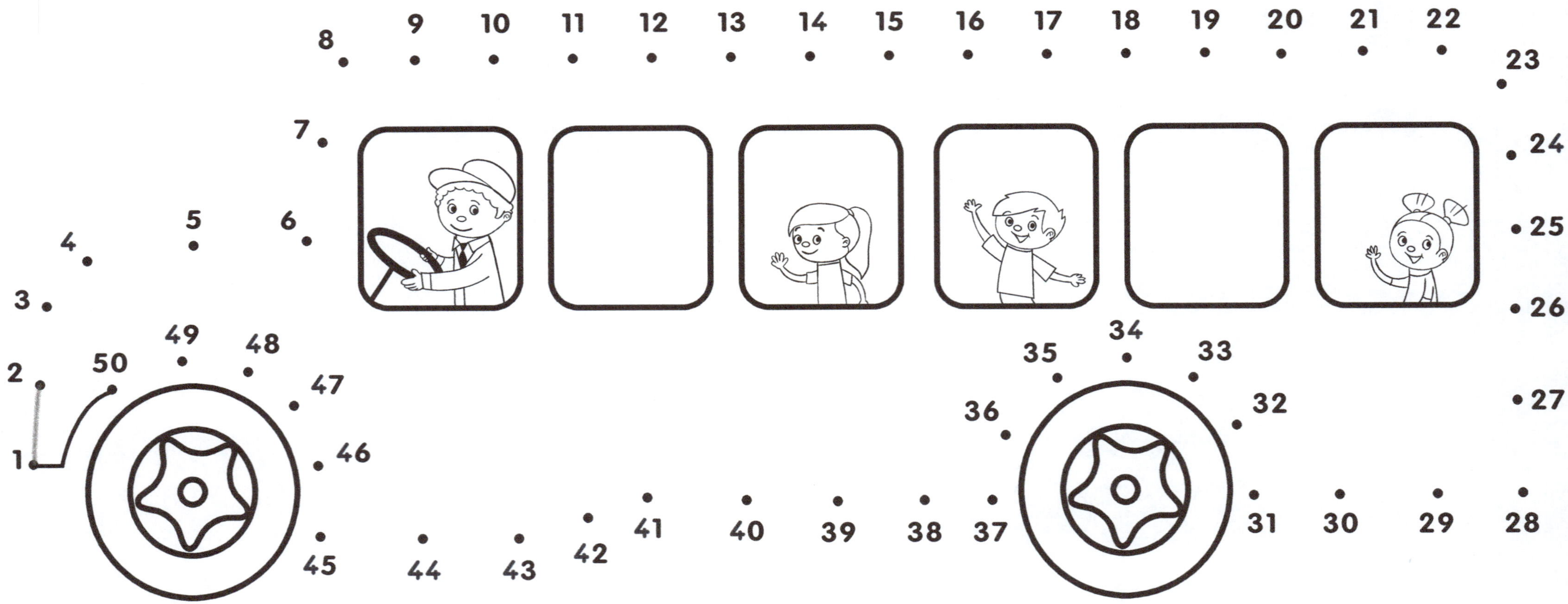

Connect the dots to complete the picture. Point and say.
Language: numbers 1–50

Shapes

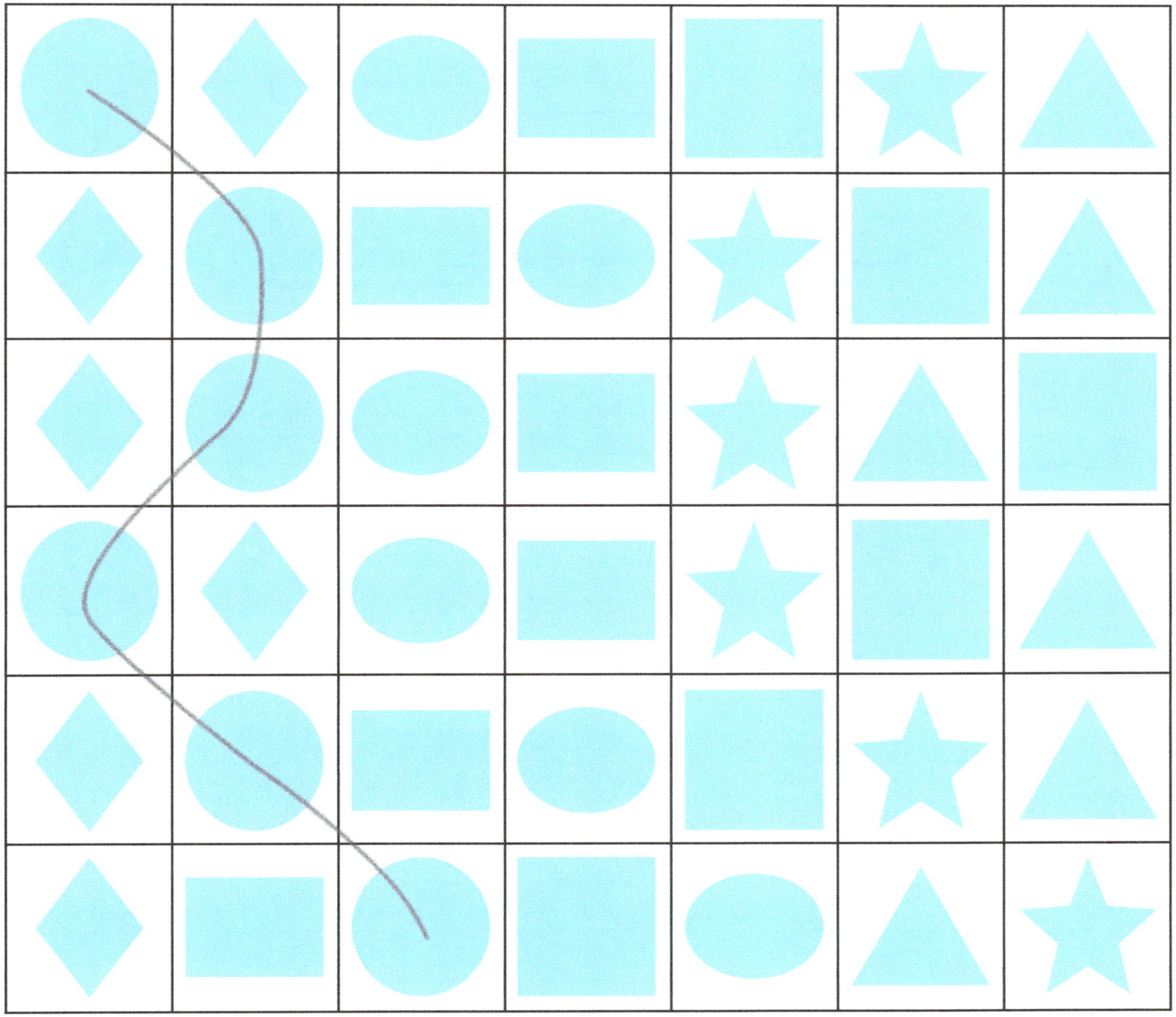

Draw a line to follow each shape in the grid. Point and say.
Language: circle, diamond, oval, rectangle, square, star, triangle; It's (a star).

Shapes

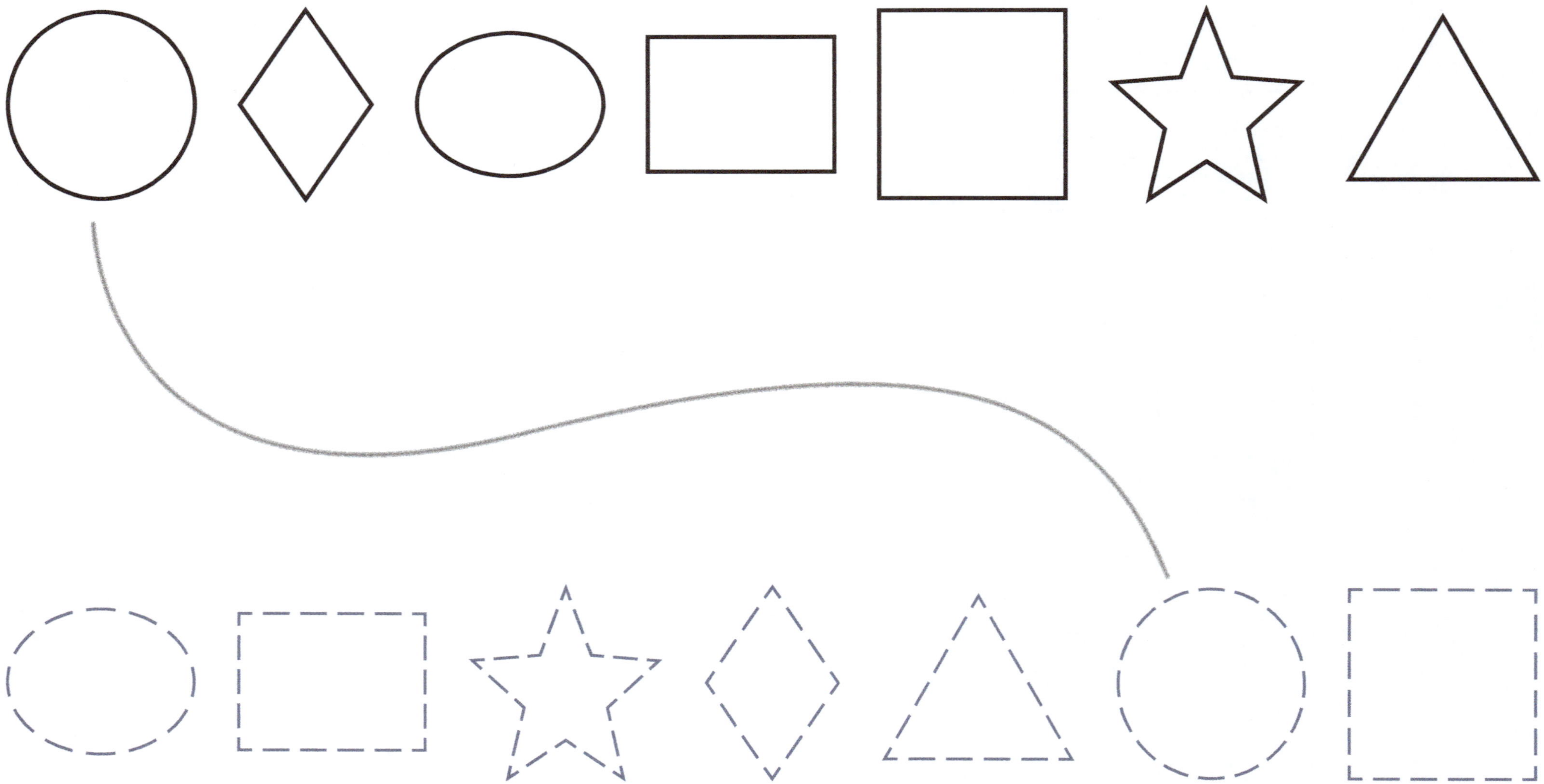

Trace and match the shapes. Color the pairs of shapes the same color. Point and say.
Language: circle, diamond, oval, rectangle, square, star, triangle; colors; It's (a star). It's (red).

Concepts

Draw pictures to show food and drink for when you're hungry and thirsty. Point and say.
Language: hungry, thirsty; drink, food; I'm (hungry). I like (apples).

Concepts

Color the frames of the pictures that show clean green. Color the frames of the pictures that show dirty red. Point and say.
Language: clean, dirty; It's (clean).

Concepts

Find and circle the old people and animals green. Find and circle the young people and animals red. Point and say.
Language: old, young; He's/She's/It's (old).

Festivals

World Book Day

Draw and color your favorite book. Point and say.
Language: animals, people, pictures, stories, words, world; I like books with (stories). I like books about (the world).

World Animal Day

Look and match. Draw and color to complete the animals. Circle your favorite animal. Point and say.
Language: elephant, gorilla, panda, polar bear, rhino, tiger; I like the (rhino). Save the (panda).

Festivals

World Environment Day

Follow and draw the paths from the children to the places.
Color your favorite place. Point and say.
Language: beach, countryside, forest, mountains; I go to the (countryside).